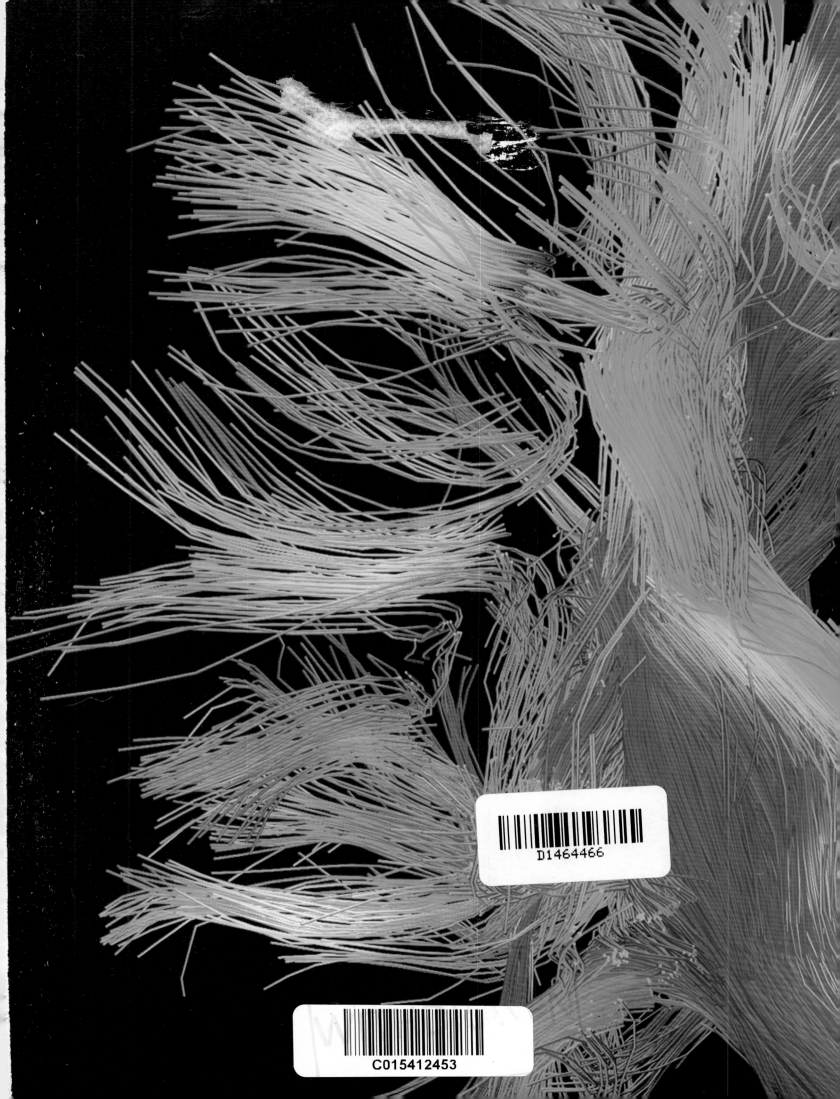

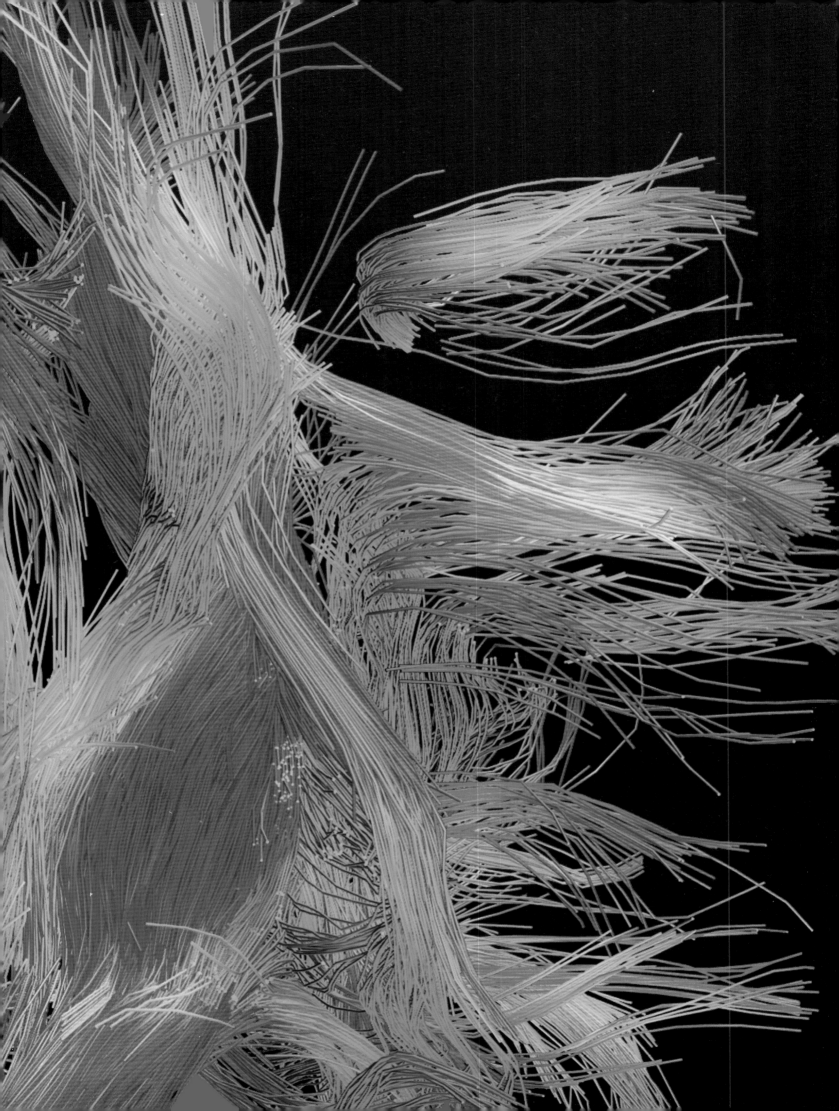

MUSE

THE 2ND LAW

© 2012 by Faber Music Ltd
First published by Faber Music Ltd in 2012
Bloomsbury House
74–77 Great Russell Street
London WC1B 3DA

Music Arranged by Olly Weeks
Edited by Lucy Holliday

Book Design by Chloë Alexander
Neuro images supplied courtesy of the Human Connectome Project,
Laboratory of Neuro Imaging, UCLA
Band Photography by Gavin Bond

Printed in England by Caligraving Ltd

This paper is 100% recyclable

ISBN10: 0-571-53737-5
EAN13: 978-0-571-53737-2

To buy Faber Music publications or to find out about the full range of titles available,
please contact your local music retailer or Faber Music sales enquiries:

Faber Music Limited, Burnt Mill, Elizabeth Way, Harlow CM20 2HX
Tel: +44 (0)1279 82 89 82
Fax: +44 (0)1279 82 89 83
sales@fabermusic.com
fabermusicstore.com

musemanagement.co.uk
muse.mu

Contents

SUPREMACY

Words and Music by Matthew Bellamy

Wake to see, your true e - man - ci - pa - tion is a

fan - ta - sy._____

Your su - pre - ma - cy.__

MADNESS

Words and Music by Matthew Bellamy

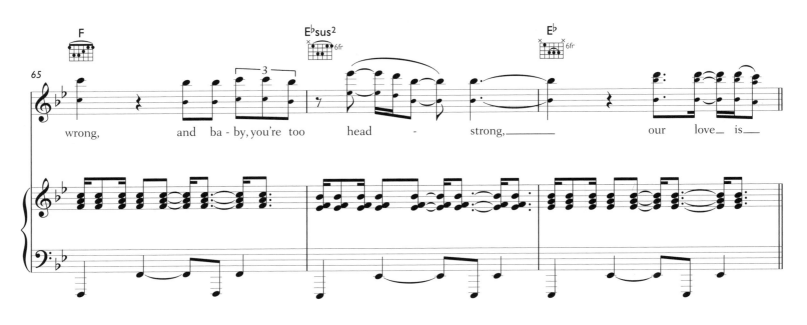

PANIC STATION

Words and Music by Matthew Bellamy

1. You won't get much clos-er___ un-til you sac-ri-fice it all,
2. Doubts will try to break you,___ un - leash your heart and soul,

you won't get to taste it___ with your
troub-le will sur-round you,___ start

face a-gainst the wall,
tak-ing some con-trol,

get up and com-mit, show___ the
stand up and de-li-ver___ your

po-wer trapped with-in,
wild-est fan-ta-sy,

do

PRELUDE

Words and Music by Matthew Bellamy

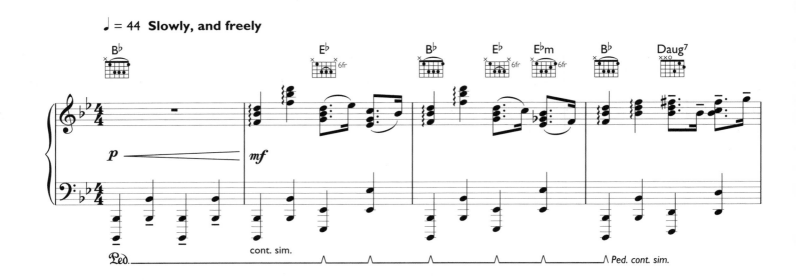

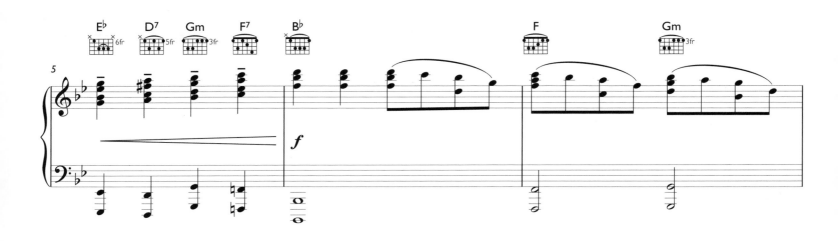

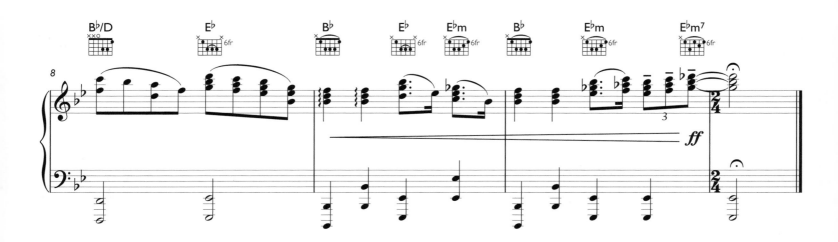

SURVIVAL

Words and Music by Matthew Bellamy

FOLLOW ME

Words and Music by Matthew Bellamy

When dark-ness falls and sur-rounds you, when you fall down, when you're scared and you're lost. Be

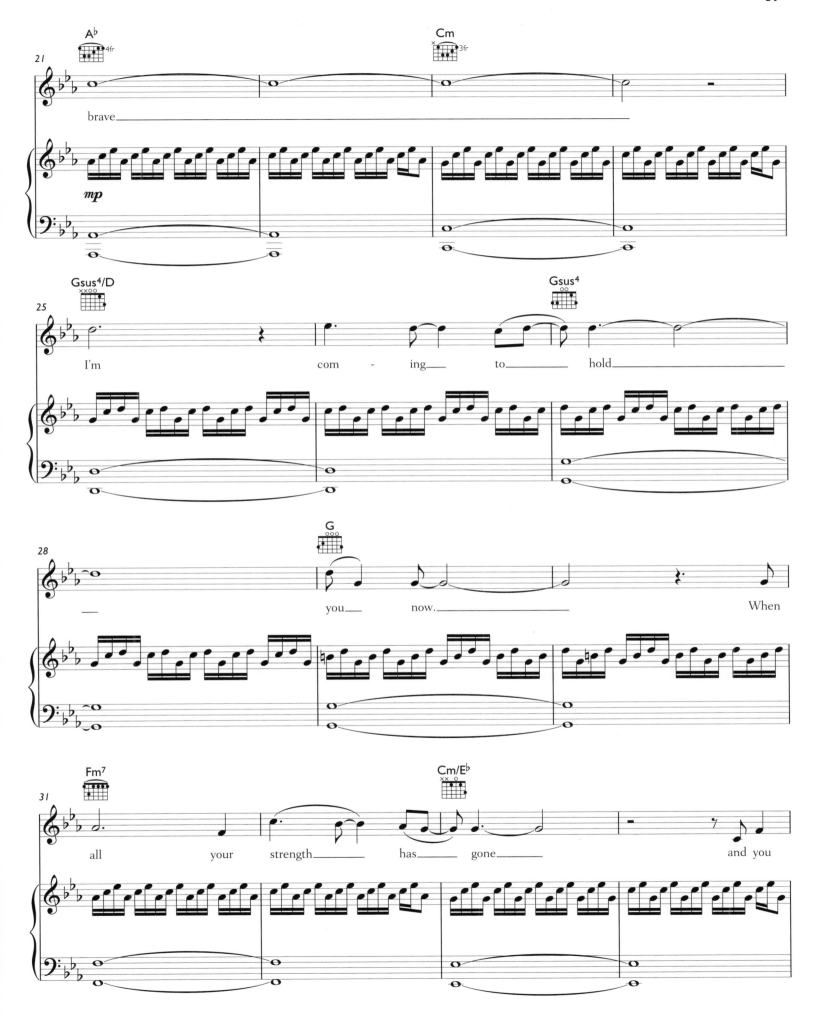

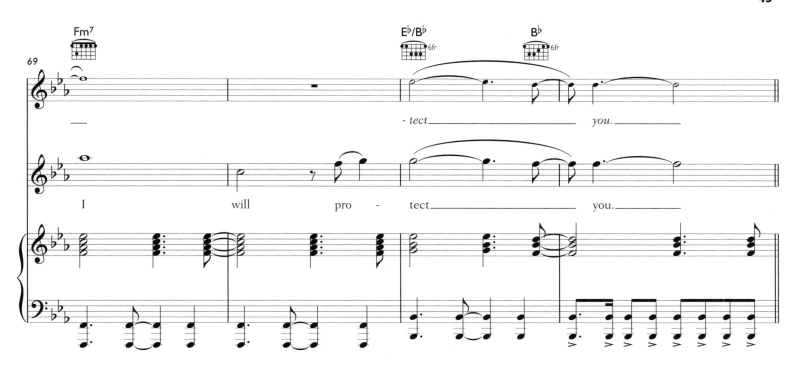

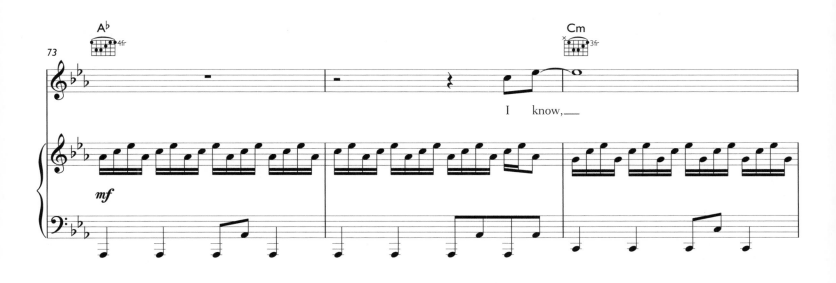

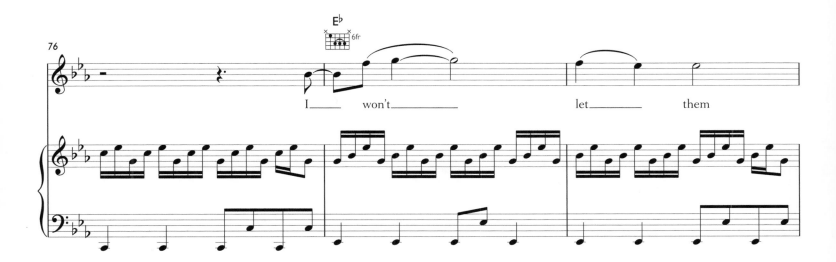

(Ah,_____ ah,_____

Fol - low_ me,_____ you can_ fol - low_ me,_____

ah,_____

I_ will al-ways keep_ you_____ safe._

Fol - low_ me,_____ ah,_____ you can_ trust in me,_____ ah,_____

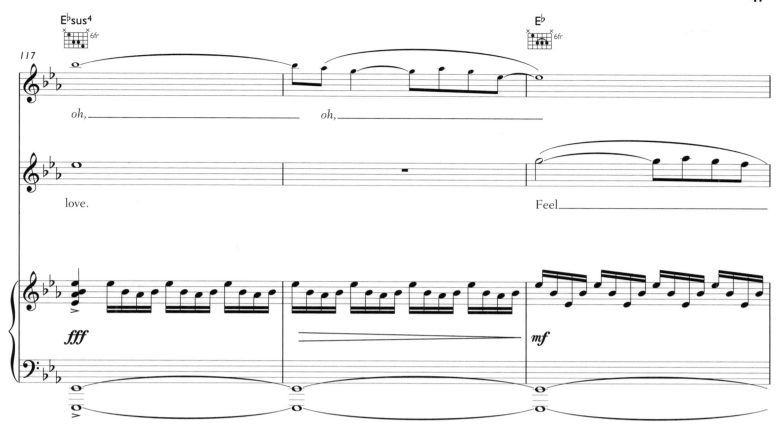

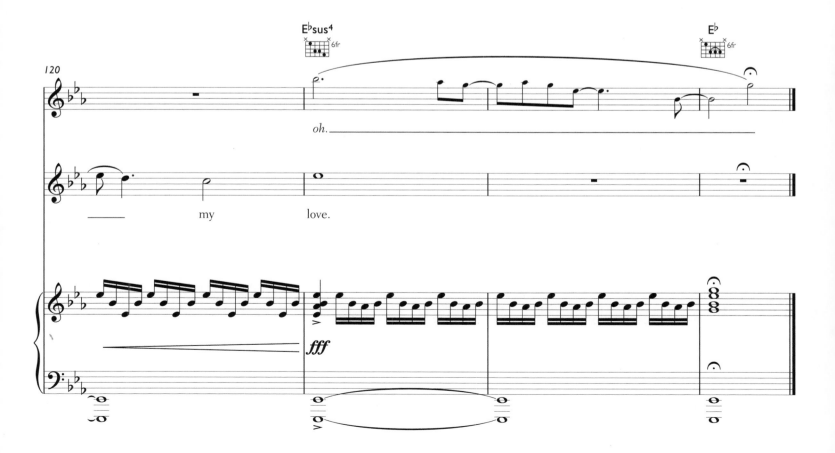

ANIMALS

Words and Music by Matthew Bellamy

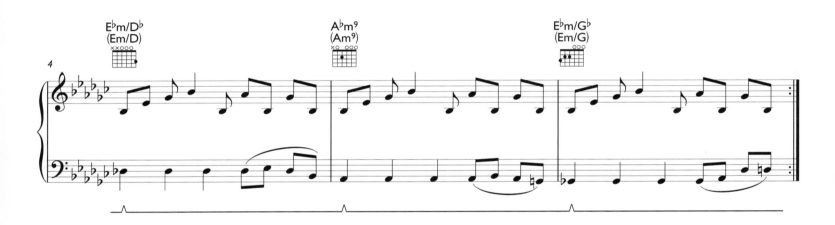

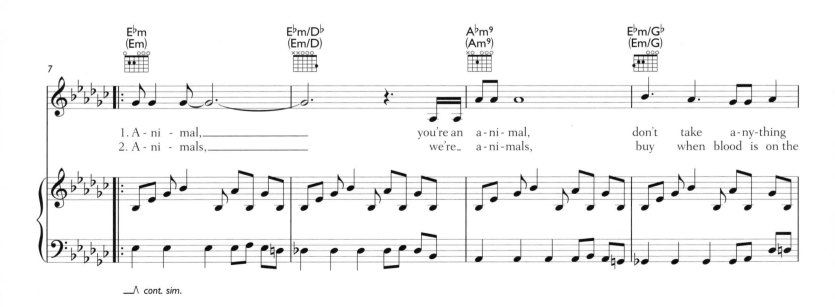

1. A-ni - mal, you're an a-ni-mal, don't take a-ny-thing
2. A-ni - mals, we're a-ni-mals, buy when blood is on the

cont. sim.

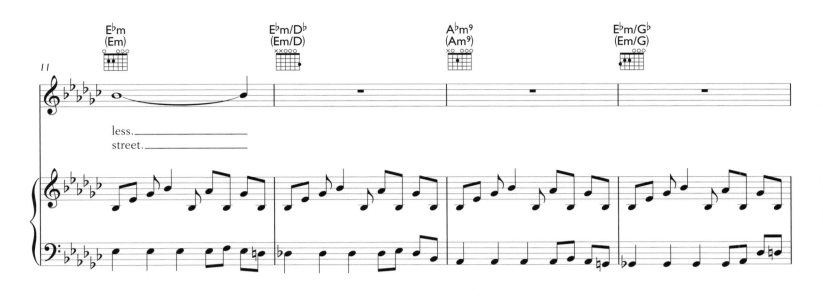

less._____
street._____

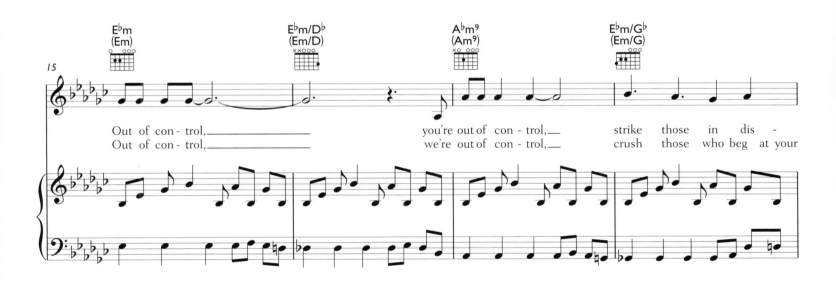

Out of con - trol,_____ you're out of con - trol,___ strike those in dis -
Out of con - trol,_____ we're out of con - trol,___ crush those who beg at your

- tress._____
feet._____

Wall Street trading floor samples

N.C.

EXPLORERS

Words and Music by Matthew Bellamy

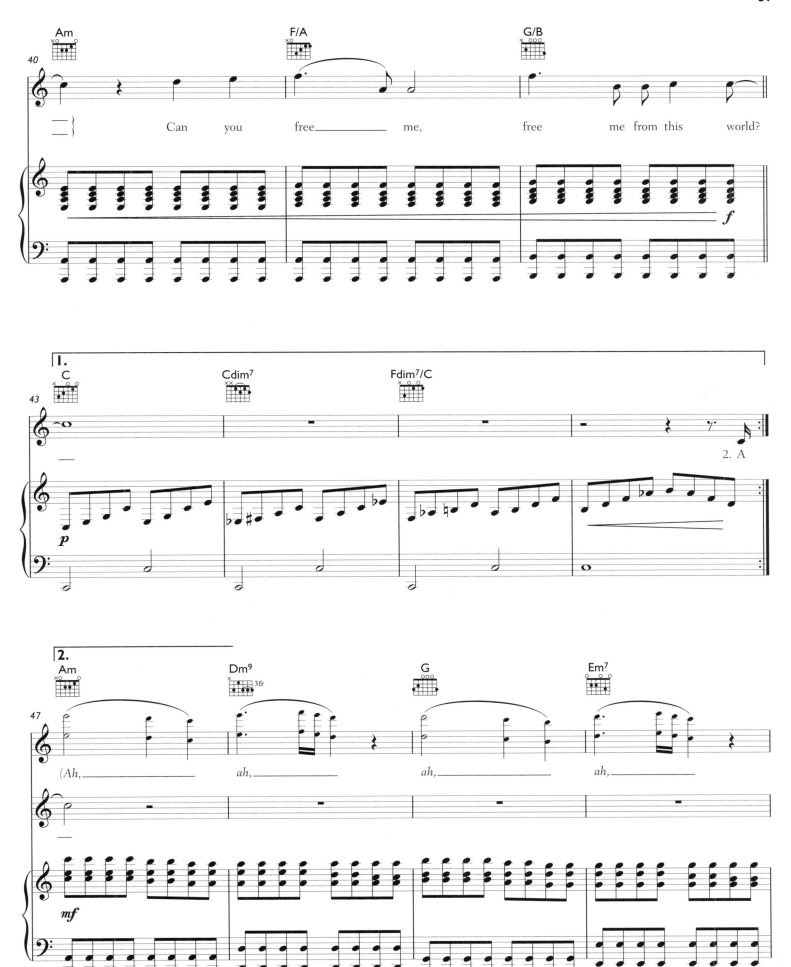

Can you free_____ me, free me from this world?

(Ah,_____ ah,_____ ah,_____ ah,_____

-long____ here,   it { was a mis-take____ im-pri-son-ing____ my soul.__
run-ning a-round____ in circles feeling caged by end - less rules. }

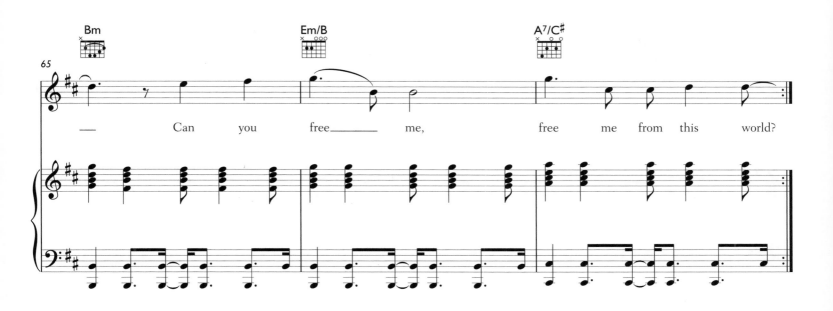

__   Can you free____ me,   free me from this world?

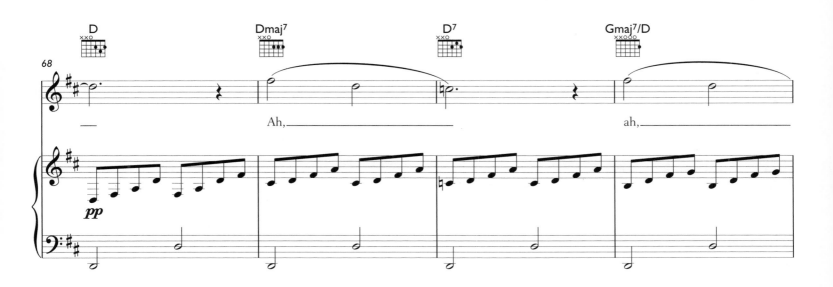

_   Ah,_____   ah,_____

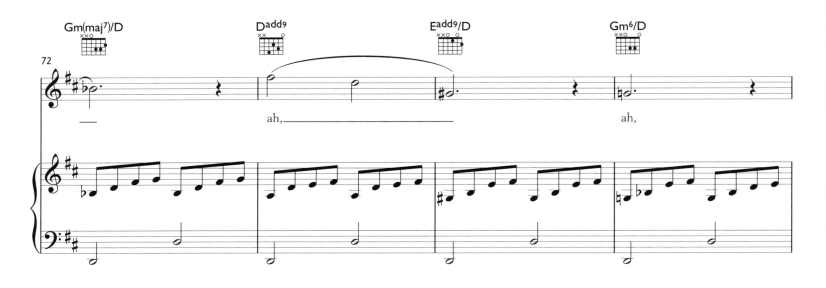

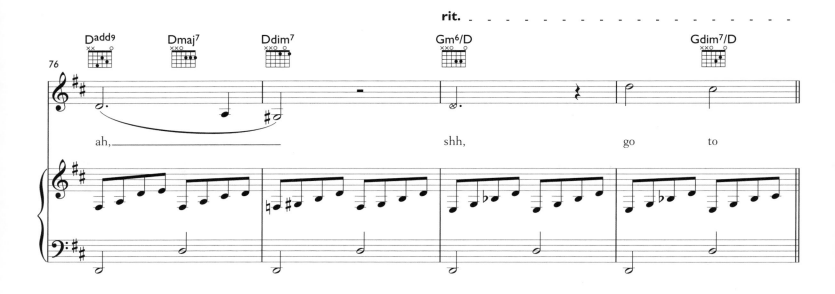

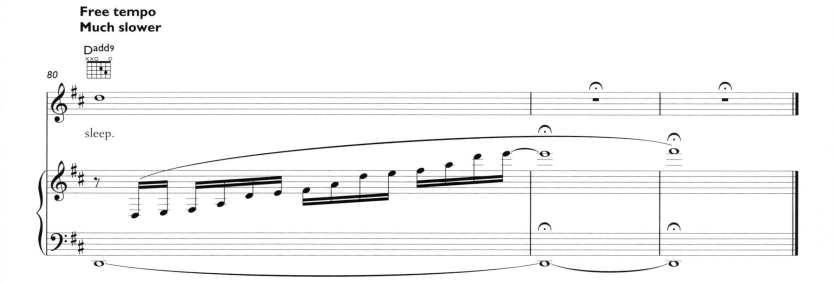

BIG FREEZE

Words and Music by Matthew Bellamy

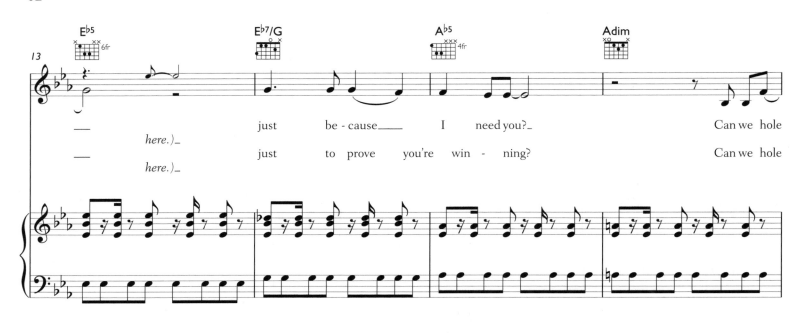

just be-cause___ I need you?___ Can we hole
just to prove you're win-ning? Can we hole

here.)
here.)

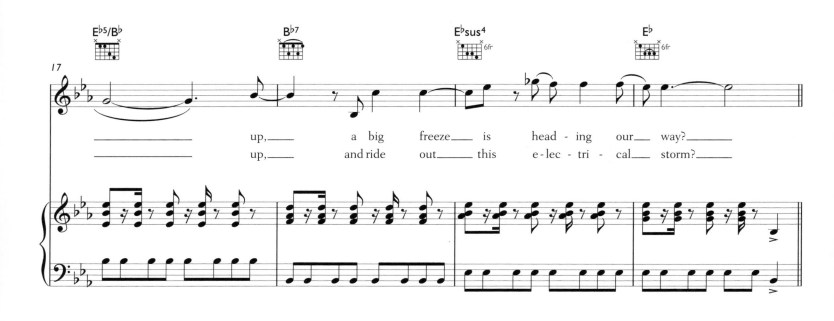

_____ up,___ a big freeze___ is head-ing our___ way?_____
_____ up,___ and ride out___ this e-lec-tri-cal___ storm?_____

We are on a hid-ing to no-where, we still hope,
We des-troyed some-thing beautiful, we have faith,

_f_

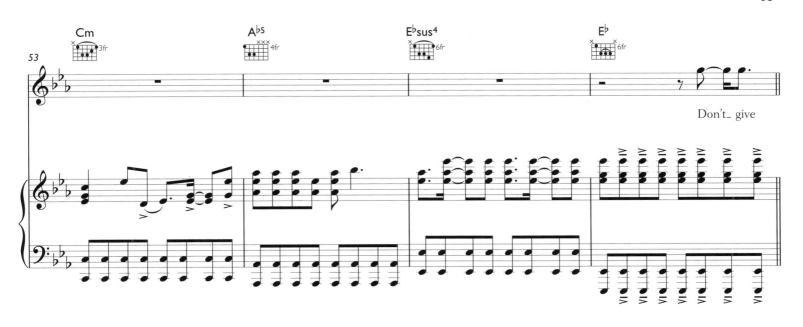

Don't_ give

up, don't let the ma - gic__ leave_ us,__ we're col -lap-

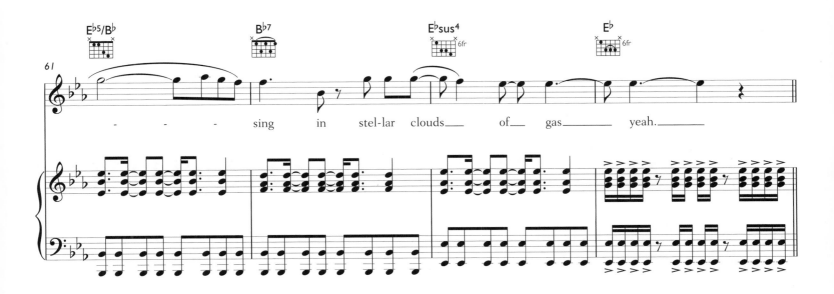

- - - sing in stel-lar clouds__ of_ gas___ yeah.___

feel_____ me,_____ I won't let____ the sun in your heart de-cay.

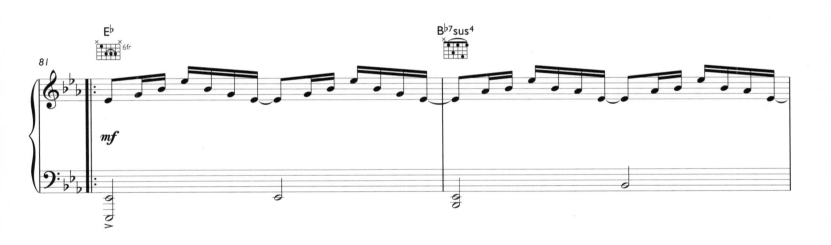

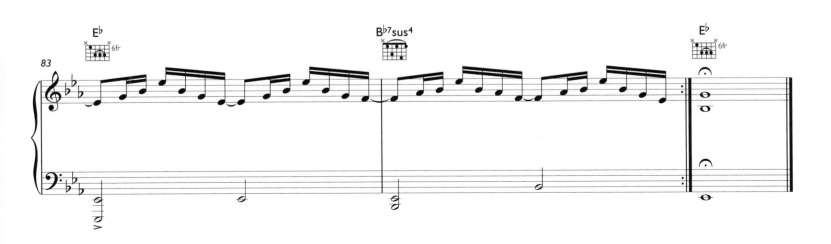

SAVE ME

Words and Music by Chris Wolstenholme

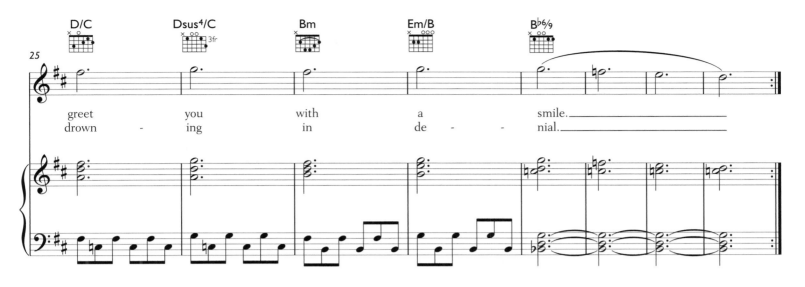

greet   you   with   a   smile._____

drown - ing   with   in   de - nial._____

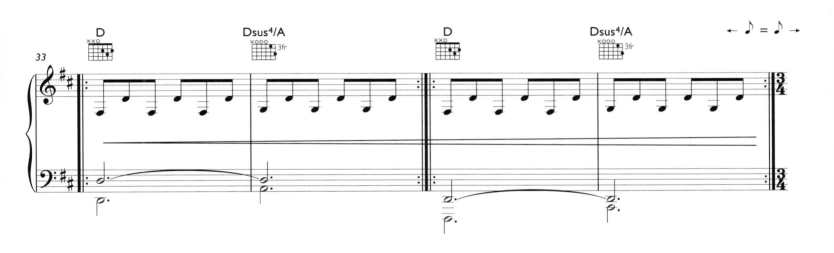

2. (Run   a - - way   and

1. Turn   me   in - - to

2. Run   a - - way   and

I need your res - - cue.)

that we can go to,
I need your res - - cue.____

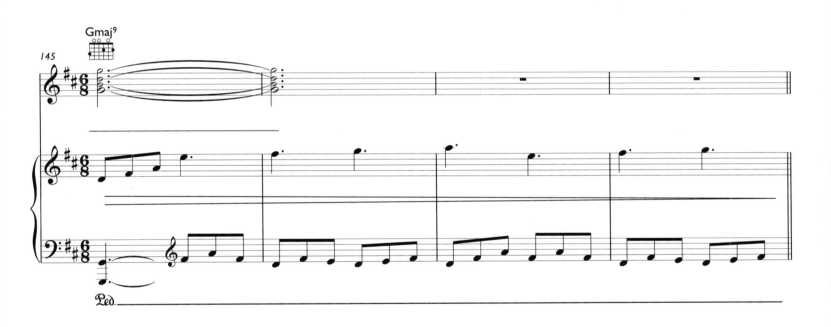

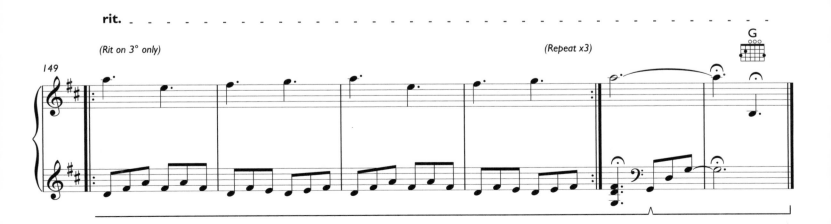

rit. _ rit. _ _ _ _ _

(Rit on 3° only)   (Repeat x3)

LIQUID STATE

Words and Music by Chris Wolstenholme

THE 2ND LAW: UNSUSTAINABLE

Words and Music by Matthew Bellamy

(Spoken:) "All virtual and technological processes proceed in such a way that the availability of the

remaining energy decreases. In all energy exchanges, if no energy enters or leaves an isolated system

Un-sus-tain - er, un-sus-tain - er.

Oh, _____ oh, _____ oh, _____

oh, _____ oh. _____

(Spoken:) *"The*

fundamental laws of thermodynamics will place fixed limits on technological innovation and human advancement.

THE 2ND LAW: ISOLATED SYSTEM

Words and Music by Matthew Bellamy

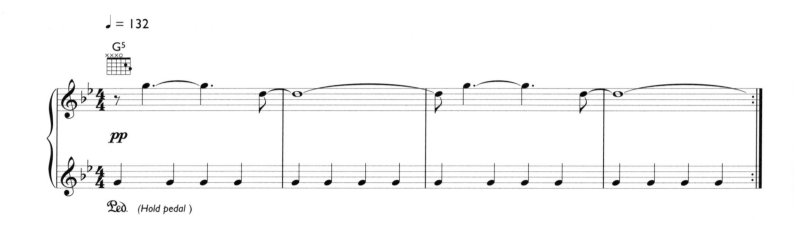

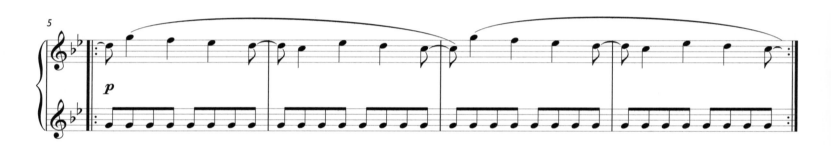

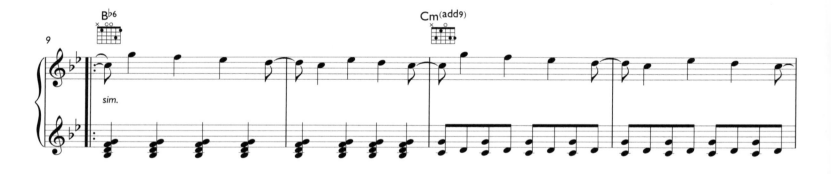

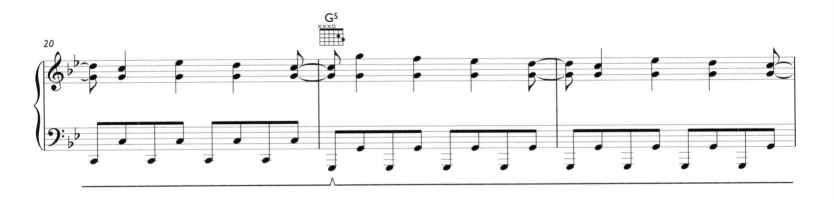